Lynn Kyle's Photoshop Training Course
Workbook

Prepared and presented by

L YNN K YLE

Pearson PTR Interactive
Photoshop Video Course

Prentice Hall PTR
Upper Saddle River, New Jersey 07458

Table of Contents

LECTURE 1   Photoshop Review   1

LECTURE 2   Preparing Images for the Web   16

LECTURE 3   Transparency   31

LECTURE 4   Creating Background Graphics and Effects   37

LECTURE 5   Creative Text Effects   48

LECTURE 6   Navigation, Buttons, and Bullets   67

LECTURE 7   Inline Graphics   79

LECTURE 8   ImageReady: Springboard to the Web   101

LECTURE 9   Real-Life Example: A Complete Walkthrough   130

Lecture One

Photoshop Review

Objectives:

- Preview Lecture 1

- Tour New Features in Photoshop 5.5 and 6.0

- Tour the Photoshop 6.0 Toolbar

- Explore the Photoshop 6.0 Palettes and Learn Palette Changes in Version 6

- Create, Delete, and Rename Layers

- Manage Multiple Layers

- Merge, Link, Move, View, and Flatten Layers

- Create and Batch Actions

- Explore More Ins and Outs of Actions

- Understand Photoshop Color

- Explore the History Palette

- Review Lecture 1

The Upgrade From 5 to 5.5

The ImageReady Addition
Adobe's ImageReady, a specifically Web-based program, now comes bundled with the Photoshop software.

Easier Optimization
Photoshop makes optimizing your JPEG and GIF files more convenient.

New Masking Tools
The two new Eraser tools and the Extract function make creating transparencies so easy that the GIF 89a format has become obsolete.

Enhanced Color Picker
Getting both a hexadecimal value and a Web-safe color are convenient and easy in the new Color Picker.

Better Text Features

Picture Package
Photoshop will lay out one image in various configurations on an 8.5" x 11" page.

The Upgrade From 5.5 to 6
Here are some of the major changes:

- *The Options Palette*
- *The Layers Palette*
- *The Text Editor*
- *Liquify*
- *The Slice and Slice Selection Tools*
- *Saving Files*
- *Easier Color Management*
- *Increased User Friendliness*

Notes:

_____

_____

The Toolbar

Selection Tools

🔲 **Elliptical and Rectangular Marquees**

🔲 **Row and Column Marquees**

🔲 **Crop**

🔲 **Magic Wand**

🔲 **Free-Form and Polygon Lassos**

🔲 **Magnetic Lasso**

🔲 **Move**

🔲 **Airbrush**

🔲 **Paintbrush**

🔲 **Rubber Stamp: Clone and Pattern**

🔲 **History Brush**

🔲 **Art History Brush**

🔲🔲 **Note Tool**

🔲🔲🔲 **Shape Tool**

🔲🔲🔲

🔲🔲 **Slice Tool**

🔲**Eraser**

🔲 **Line**

Notes:

_____

_____

_____

- Pencil
- Smudge
- Blur
- Sharpen
- Burn
- Dodge
- Sponge
- Pen
- Magnetic Pen
- Free Form Pen
- Plus and Minus Pens
- Arrow Tool
- Convert-Anchor-Point Tool
- Type

Ruler

- Gradient
- Paintbucket
- Eyedropper and Color Sampler
- Hand
- Magnifying Glass
- Colors

Edit Modes

View Modes

Notes:

_____

_____

Palettes

- **The Navigator Palette**

  Navigate through portions of your image.

- **Info Palette**

  Provides information on relative color values, the location of your mouse pointer, the width and height of any selection, and the angle and distance of measurements being made.

- **The Options Palette**

  Each tool has its own Options palette.

- **Color Palette**

  Choose a specific foreground or background color.

- **Swatches Palette**

  Save specific shades that you create for later use.

- **Brushes Palette**

  Displays all the available brushes (by size, style, and shape) for your current painting/drawing tool.

- **Layers Palette**

  Allows you to add to your image on one layer without affecting portions of your image on other layers.

- **Channels Palette**

  Acts as a storage area for image color and saved selections, and allows you to create effects with masks.

- **Paths Palette**

  This palette (used with the Pen tool) retains path information and allows for path adjustments.

- **History Palette**

  This palette saves a preset number of moves and changes to your image.

- **Actions Palette**

  This palette creates and remembers sequences of actions as macros so you can easily reproduce these sequences.

Notes:

_____

_____

Working with Layers

Creating and Deleting Layers

Figure 1–20 shows and describes the Layers palette, while Figure 1–21 graphically illustrates layers.

To add a new layer to your image, you have a number of choices, including:

- Place text on your canvas, or paste something from the clipboard into your image.
- Push the Create New Layer icon.
- In the Layers palette menu, choose New Layer.
- From the menu bar, choose Layers → New → Layer.

To delete a layer, you do one of the following three things:

- Simply drag the layer to the garbage can in the lower right corner of the Layers palette
- From the Layers palette menu, choose Delete Layer
- From the menu bar, choose Layer → Delete Layer

Notes:

_____

_____

_____

_____

_____

_____

_____

Renaming Layers

In a multilayered image, it is easy to lose track of which layers hold which specific objects. Therefore, give each layer a name which helps describe what is in that layer.

Managing Multiple Layers

Photoshop 6 now provides the ability to create Layer sets. Creating a set, which you can do by clicking the Layer set icon at the bottom of your Layers palette, is like creating a folder or directory in your Layers palette.

Moving, Linking, and Merging Layers

To merge the contents of two or more layers into a single layer, the following options are offered to you in the Layers palette or menu bar Layer menus:

- If your layers are linked, choose Merge Linked.
- To merge your layer with the layer below the active layer, choose Merge Down.
- If any of your layers are turned off (see below), choose Merge Visible.

Notes:

_____

_____

_____

_____

_____

_____

Viewing Layers: Turning Them On or Off

You can turn a layer on or off by clicking on the Eye icon on the left-side column.

Flattening Layers

To flatten all layers, choose Flatten Image from either the Layers palette menu or the menu bar Layer menu.

Notes:

_____

_____

_____

_____

_____

_____

_____

_____

_____

_____

_____

_____

_____

Saving Time with Actions

By recording actions, you can perform a complex set of functions that can replay repeatedly through any number of images.

Creating Actions

To create a new Action:

1. In the Action menu options, choose New Action. Give your new Action a name.
2. Perform the functions you wish to be the components of your new Action.
3. When you have finished all the individual functions that make up your new Action, push the Stop icon at the bottom of the Actions palette.
6. Play your action by either pushing the Play icon at the bottom of the Actions palette.

The Action "plays" without you having to go through each step.

Notes:

_____

_____

_____

_____

_____

_____

_____

_____

Batching Actions

Use the batch option to perform your action on a folder full of images.

1. Simply select your desired action and choose File → Automate → Batch.
2. Select the folder where all the images on which you want to run this action are located.
3. Click "OK."

The chosen Action will be performed on all images in the folder.

Notes:

_____

_____

_____

_____

_____

_____

_____

_____

_____

_____

_____

_____

Viewing an Action Before Completion

To program an Action to stop at some point before completion (perhaps to judge its progress), choose Insert Stop from the Actions palette menu.

Forcing Menu Items to Work

Force the Actions palette to recognize otherwise grayed-out commands by choosing Insert Menu Option from the Actions palette pull-down menu.

Changing the Look of the Palette

To turn an Action into a button, make sure you are not currently recording an action and choose Button Mode from the pull-down menu.

Creating and Saving Sets

To begin a set of Actions, choose New Set from the Actions palette pull-down menu. You can create new actions within this set, or you can move already existing actions into it.

To save a set, click on the set name and choose Save Actions from the palette pull-down menu.

To use a set, simply choose Load Actions from the palette pull-down menu.

Notes:

_____

_____

_____

_____

_____

_____

Photoshop Color

It always helps to have a basic working knowledge of color issues you may face as you work with Photoshop and the Internet.

Color Modes

The modes you'll be concentrating on for Web design are RGB and grayscale.

- **RGB** is the mode in which you will usually create and manipulate your images. This is different from CMYK, the mode used for printed material.
- **Grayscale** allows you to work only in shades of gray.

The Color Picker

Clicking on either the foreground or background color in the toolbar gives you access to the Color Picker.

Notes:

_____

_____

_____

_____

_____

_____

_____

_____

_____

The History Palette

The main function of the History palette is to provide for multiple undos. It also allows you to experiment in ways you never could before.

The History Palette

By clicking on any title in the palette, your image will go back to that state.

Settings

The following options will be available to you:

- Maximum History States
- Automatically Create First Snapshot
- Allow Non-Linear History

If you want to change the number of history states, choose Edit → Preferences → General Preferences.

Bad Things Happen...

There are some negatives that are associated with the History palette, the two most prominent of which are:

- **Memory Hogging:** The History palette takes up *a lot* of memory.
- **Overconfidence:** The History Pallette cannot save you from all mistakes. In particular, if Photoshop or your computer itself crashes, all the history is lost.

The History Brush

While clicking on one of the titles in the History palette will bring your image back to that entire state, the History brush will do the same, but only for the portions of your image that you paint over.

Notes:

_____

_____

SUMMARY

Notes:

_____

_____

_____

_____

_____

_____

_____

_____

_____

_____

_____

_____

_____

_____

_____

_____

Lecture 1 Exercises: Photoshop Review

1. Open the files BOSTON.JPG and BOSTON2.JPG, located under Resources on the CD-ROM. Using BOSTON.JPG as your starting point, alter the file so that it looks approximately like BOSTON2.JPG when you are finished. This exercise concentrates on having you practice using the tools on the Photoshop 6 toolbar. Be sure not to leave any hard edges in the final picture. Save your work as EX1_1.JPG.

2. Set your monitor resolution to 800 x 600. Open the Options palette, then drag the tab of any other open palettes into the Options palette's Palette Well. Get used to using the Palette Well to save screen real estate.

3. Open the files STATEHOUSE.JPG and SUNSCAPE.JPG. Use the Magic Erase tool to remove the sky from STATEHOUSE.JPG. Cut a large portion of SUNSCAPE.JPG and paste it into STATEHOUSE.JPG. Name the layers appropriately and rearrange them so that the statehouse is in the foreground, the sunscape is in the background. Position the sunset until you are satisfied with how it looks, then link these two layers. Add a new layer with the text "Sunset in Boston." Save your work as EX1_3.JPG.

4. Create the following actions and assign a keyboard shortcut to each:
   - Add Emboss
   - Copy and Paste
   - Save and Close
   - Duplicate Layer
   - Change Hue + 30

Lecture Two

Preparing Images for the Web

Objectives:

- Preview Lecture 2

- Explore Issues Associated with Web Graphics

- Tour the Save for Web Command Center

- Manipulate GIF Settings

- Manipulate JPEG Settings

- Explore the Image Size and Color Table Tabs

- Save Images

- Review Lecture 2

Issues Associated with Web Graphics

Modem Speed

While most businesses can usually be expected to have broadband connections, this is not yet true for the average private individual. This can restrict the size and number of graphics which should be included in a Web page since slow speeds lead to long delays if a large graphic, or a large number of medium-sized graphics, are present.

Color Palettes

The use of colors is not as restricted as it used to be, and, in addition, Photoshop has added a Save For Web feature which eliminates a great deal of the difficulty which used to be associated with finding the right colors to use for your online graphics to display properly.

Browser Issues

Later Browser versions and WYSIWYG editors have made cross-browser problems with images less prevalent. Nonetheless, careful attention should be paid to the look of the images when displayed in any target browser, and the designer should be aware that the technology continues to change, and may introduce new difficulties in this area at any time.

Notes:

_____

_____

_____

_____

_____

_____

Establishing a Least Common Denominator

There are two general LCDs, one for B2B sites and one for B2C (business-to-consumer) sites. These change as the technology advances, always increasing, and vary also with target market.

B2B Sites:
ISDN, 800 x 600 monitor resolution, IE 4 browser

B2C Sites:
36.6 modem, 800 x 600 monitor resolution, IE 4 browser

Note that the only difference between the two here is the connection speed. This is a very large difference, however, in terms of what size of graphic can be reasonably supported by the site.

Notes:

_____

_____

_____

_____

_____

_____

_____

_____

_____

_____

File Types for the Web

When it comes to flat, 2D images, there are really only two file formats to consider: JPEG and GIF. While other formats, such as PNG, have been proposed as standards, they have failed to make significant inroads on the Web display front. The features of the two formats, which determine which you choose for a given image, are:

- **GIF:** Uses a color index and supports up to 256 colors (8-bit color); can be transparent and made into basic animations; uses lossless compression. GIFs are best when there are specific details of the image which are necessary for the success of the piece.
- **JPEG:** Supports up to 16 million colors (24-bit); cannot be made transparent; lossy compression. JPEGs are best when you are dealing with photographs or other images that use a large number of colors and shadings.

Notes:

_____

_____

_____

_____

_____

_____

_____

_____

_____

Saving GIFs and JPEGs for the Web

Access the "Save for Web" choice through the File Menu. This will bring up a large dialogue box with several important parts: the Preview Window, the Toolbar, the Preview Menu, OK/Cancel Buttons, Output Settings, and Settings.

Preview Window

While this has four choices available—Original, Optimized, 2-Up, and 4-Up—4-Up is the most commonly used and recommended because it permits the greatest range of comparison between variants of the original image. This choice displays four separate images—the original in the upper left corner and three other "working" versions which can be modified.

Toolbar

Contains the Hand, Zoom, and Eyedropper tools. Hand and Zoom apply to all four images simultaneously.

Preview Menu

This permits you to view the image according to browser, platform, and connection speed.

OK and Cancel Buttons

Notes:

_____

_____

_____

_____

_____

_____

Output Settings Button

The pull-down menu at the top of the dialog box is set to HTML by default, but also lets you change settings for the Background, Saving Files, and Slices.

5. HTML
Allows you to format your HTML in specific ways that are more consistent with how you write HTML yourself.

6. Saving Files
Allows you to set conventions for naming files and placing them in folders.

7. Slices
Allows you to work with slices if you created them in Photoshop. See Lecture 8 for more details.

Notes:

_____

_____

_____

_____

_____

_____

_____

_____

_____

Settings

Permits you to change various parameters on the currently selected one of the three working images in the Preview window. Click on one of the three working images to make it the current selection.

The Optimize Menu

Has the following three options:

8. Save or Delete Settings

Allows you to keep sets of settings that you find useful and to remove them later.

9. Optimize to File Size

Permits you to select a desired size of file and let Photoshop create a version of your image which saves as many of your other settings as possible.

10. Repopulate Views

Choose this when you want to start from scratch, and have Photoshop provide optimization values for all quadrants in the Save as Web dialog box.

Notes:

_____

_____

_____

_____

_____

_____

_____

The GIF Settings

- ***Color Reduction Algorithm***

    Lets you choose the palette for your image. Has several choices:

    - *System (Windows or Macintosh)*

        Will use either the Windows or Macintosh default 8-bit color palette, respectively.

    - *Web*

        Saves your image with the browser-safe web colors.

    - *Adaptive*

        Analyzes your image and creates a palette consisting of the best colors for that image.

    - *Custom*

        The custom method lets you use your own palette for your image.

    - *Previous*

        This feature lets you use the same palette on multiple images. You must have already converted an image using either the adaptive or custom method.

Notes:

_____

_____

_____

_____

_____

_____

_____

- *Dithering Algorithm*

    Dithering permits Photoshop to use a limited number of colors to create the illusion of more colors. Different algorithms do this in different ways.

- *Transparency*

    Activates or deactivates Transparent parts of the image.

- *Interlacing*

    An interlaced image loads a rough, blurry version first and then loads the details. Commonly used for larger images on the Web.

- *Lossy*

    Compresses the image more at the cost of some details/lost color. Cannot be used with Noise or Pattern Dither or with Interlacing.

- *Colors*

    Choose how many colors the image uses.

- *Dither*

    Select the percentage of dither used for the Diffusion Dither algorithm.

- *Matte*

    If you have transparency in your image, and the Transparency checkbox is not clicked, the Matte color will replace the transparent areas with the selected colors. If the Transparency checkbox is clicked, the Matte color you choose will place a thin border of your selected color around the edges of your images.

- *Web Snap*

    The Web Snap feature allows you to control the amount of browser dither.

Notes:

_____

_____

_____

_____

The JPEG Settings

- *Compression Quality*

  Use this pull-down menu to choose the amount of compression for your image quickly.

- *Progressive*

  Like interlacing: loads a rough blurry version quickly then works on adding detail.

- *ICC Profile*

  The ICC (International Color Consortium) profile format assists you in recreating the same colors in your image from one platform to another.

- *Optimized*

  Click on this checkbox to enhance your image but also reduce your file size. Some browsers may not read this type of image.

- *Quality*

  Choose the quality of the image here. Higher quality, bigger file size.

- *Blur*

  Reduce the number of colors by blurring the whole image.

- *Matte*

  Selects the color which will replace transparent portions of your image (since JPEGs do not support transparency).

Notes:

_____

_____

_____

_____

_____

_____

Lower Tabs

Image Size Tab
Allows you to resize images. Works on all three working images at once. Choose method Photoshop uses to accomplish the change in size:

- *Bicubic* for the smoothest but slowest resize
- *Bilinear* for the fastest resize
- *Nearest neighbor* to let Photoshop delete or duplicate pixels as it feels necessary

Color Table Tab
Displays all the colors that would be used in the GIF version of your image.

- **Sorting Colors**
  Sort colors to your specifications.
- **Adding Colors**
  If your image has fewer than 256 colors, you may add colors.
- **Selecting, Editing, and Changing Colors**
  - With the Eyedropper tool, click a color in your image. The corresponding color swatch in the Color table will indicate that it has been selected with a white border.
  - Click the desired color in the Color table. Hold the Shift key down and select another color. All colors in between will be selected as well. To select two or more colors without the colors in between being selected, make your selections while holding the Command (Ctrl in Windows) key.
  - Choose Select All Colors from the Color table pull-down menu.
  - To select all Web-safe colors that appear in the table, choose Select All Web Safe Colors from the pull-down menu, or choose Select All Non-Web Safe Colors for the opposite selection.

To change a color in your image, double-click on the selected color to access the Color Picker. Select a color from the picker to replace the selected colors in your Color table.

- **Locking Colors**
  1. Use the methods described earlier in this section to select one or more colors that you want to lock.
  2. Click the Lock icon or choose Lock/Unlock Selected Colors from the Table menu.
- **Deleting Colors**

  To delete a color, simply select the color in the Color table, and either click on the Trash icon at the bottom of the table or choose Delete Color from the table pull-down menu.
- **Saving an Image With Slices**

Notes:

_____

_____

_____

_____

_____

_____

_____

_____

_____

_____

_____

_____

And Rounding Up the Features...

- *Magnification*

    Allows you to change the Zoom value of all quadrants at once.

- *Info Bar*

    Gives you information regarding the RGB and hexadecimal color values of any individual pixel.

- *Browser Options*

    This pull-down menu will open your image in the browser of your choice

Notes:

_____

_____

_____

_____

_____

_____

_____

_____

_____

_____

Saving the Image

Standard save which also includes an option to save an HTML file for the image's inclusion in Web pages.

SUMMARY

Notes:

_____

_____

_____

_____

_____

_____

_____

_____

_____

_____

_____

_____

_____

_____

_____

_____

Lecture 2 Exercises: Preparing Images for the Web

1. Open a picture file and select File → Save for Web. Click on 4-Up. Spend some time tweaking the details of your image and using the Preview menu to see the results. Be sure to select different modem speeds as well to see how your settings affect download times.

2. Open a different picture file and select File → Save for Web. Click on 4-Up. Do the same tweaking that you did in the previous exercise and observe how it affects this image.

3. Create a simple image using large red block letters on a yellow background, much like that shown in Figure 2-2. Play with the GIF dithering options to see how they affect the image. Now open a photo file containing many colors. Try setting the same dithering options as you did with the previous image to see how they affect this image.

Lecture Three

Transparency

Objectives:

- Preview Lecture 3

- Create Transparency with the Magic Eraser

- Create Transparency with the Background Eraser

- Create Transparency with the Extract Function

- Review Lecture 3

TRANSPARENCY MADE EASY

The new tools for transparency creation, the Magic Eraser, the Background Eraser, and the Extract function, each help make transparent desired portions of your image which can later be translated for direct Web use in the Save for Web dialog box.

The Magic Eraser

The Magic eraser works just like the Magic Wand tool, except that instead of creating a selection of certain pixels, it makes those pixels transparent. The Options palette for the Magic eraser tool allows you to manipulate how the tool works.

Click on the Contiguous checkbox to keep the erased pixels contiguous to the selected pixel. Click it off to allow non-contiguous pixels of the same or similar shades to be erased.

You can also manipulate how many shades of the selected color will be affected.

Notes:

_____

_____

_____

_____

_____

_____

_____

_____

The Background Eraser

To make an area of your image become transparent with the Background eraser, simply select your desired brush size and drag your mouse over the areas of your image that you wish to make transparent. The Option palette for the Background eraser allows you to choose which type of eraser you want to use:

- Find Edges will help maintain the integrity of the edges of an object, while erasing contiguous areas of the same color.
- Contiguous will erase all areas in an image that contain the selected colors that are next to each other.
- Discontiguous erases all areas in an image that contain the selected colors. These areas do not have to be next to each other or touching.

You can also choose Protect Foreground to make sure that any areas in your image that contain the foreground color will not be erased.

Notes:

_____

_____

_____

_____

_____

_____

_____

_____

Extract Image

To use the Extract Image command, follow these steps:

1. With your file open, choose Image → Extract to access the Extract dialogue box.
2. Make the Edge Highlighter tool active by clicking on it.
3. Create an edge around the object you want to extract; everything outside your edge will become transparent. If necessary, you can increase or decrease your brush size or change the color of your highlight by selecting from the Highlight pull-down menu.
4. Once you have created a highlight around the entire edge, activate the Fill tool and fill the inside of your edge selection by clicking on it. Make sure that the edge is completely closed before you click. You can change the fill color by using the Fill pull-down menu.
5. Decide how precise you would like your extraction to be by changing the Smooth slider in the Extraction area.
6. Click the Preview button to see your extracted piece. Cool, huh? Figure 3–7 shows a sample of what this should look like.
7. To see your edge highlight and fill again, click the appropriate checkboxes to make each appear. Re-edit if necessary.
8. By default, the transparent areas will appear as a checkerboard.
9. To go back to your original image, choose Original from the View pull-down menu.
10. If you already have a selection saved as an alpha channel, you can use this as a starting point.
11. Click OK.

Notes:

_____

_____

_____

_____

SUMMARY

Notes:

_____

_____

_____

_____

_____

_____

_____

_____

_____

_____

_____

_____

_____

_____

_____

Lecture 3 Exercises: Transparency

1. Open the file CAPITAL.JPG. Use the Magic Eraser tool to eliminate the sky from the image. Open the file FIREWORKS.JPG. Cut a large portion of FIREWORKS.JPG and paste it into CAPITAL.JPG. Put the fireworks in the background. Save your work as EX3_1.JPG.

2. Open the file CAPITAL.JPG. Use the Background Eraser tool to erase the background around the edges of the building. Play with the Limits and Tolerance levels to see what effects they have on the procedure. Once you've outlined the building, use the Magic Eraser tool to eliminate the rest of the sky from the image. Open the file FIREWORKS.JPG. Cut a large portion of the image and paste it into CAPITAL.JPG. Put the fireworks in the background. Save your work as EX3_2.JPG.

3. Open the file CAPITAL.JPG. Use the Extract Image tool to extract only the building from the image. Delete the remaining portions of the sky using the Magic Eraser or the Background Eraser tool. Open the file FIREWORKS.JPG. Cut a large portion of the image and paste it into CAPITAL.JPG. Put the fireworks in the background. Save your work as EX3_3.JPG.

4. Try the same procedures using REVERE.JPG instead of CAPITAL.JPG as the primary image. Get a feel for which transparency tool works best depending on the type of image with which you are working.

Lecture Four

Creating Background Graphics and Effects

Objectives:

- Preview Lecture 4

- Explore Issues Associated with Background Graphics

- Save Files as Backgrounds

- Use Hexidecimals to Create a Solid Color Background

- Create a Top Background Border

- Combine Backgrounds and Hexidecimals

- Create a Border with Shadows and Ridges

- Create Ripped or Crinkled Paper Borders

- Review Lecture 4

How Backgrounds Work in a Browser

- The background image and/or color is set in the <BODY> tag.
- The background image is the only image that can be connected to the browser window.
- The background can't be animated.
- Backgrounds don't print.
- Background images don't appear only once in the browser window. Instead, the image is placed in the top leftmost corner of the window, and tiled (repeated) infinitely down and to the right.

Notes:

_____

_____

_____

_____

_____

_____

_____

_____

_____

_____

_____

Creating Various Backgrounds

Saving Files as Backgrounds

Use one of these two methods for saving the file:

1. If you are going to use a WYSIWYG program to build your site, or code the site yourself, then use the Save for Web command that we reviewed in Chapter 2 to save your image as a GIF.
2. If you want to stay with Photoshop and ImageReady then:
    - With your image still open, launch ImageReady.
    - Within ImageReady, choose File → Output Settings → Background.
    - In the dialog box that opens, choose the radio button marked Background, and hit OK.
    - Then choose File → Save Optimized As, and name your file.

ImageReady will save your image in the format that you designate when you optimize it, and will also write and save the HTML file for you with the Background tag filled in. Open the HTML file in a browser to see what your background looks like.

Notes:

_____

_____

_____

_____

_____

_____

_____

Creating a Seamless Tiled Background

Here is an example of how to create a seamless tiled background.

1. In Photoshop, open a new file, 200 pixels wide and 200 pixels deep.
2. With black and white as your respective foreground and background colors, fill your canvas with clouds by choosing Filter → Render → Clouds.
3. Choose Filter → Other → Offset and change the settings so that your clouds are offset 100 pixels to the right and 100 pixels down.
4. Use the Rubber Stamp tool or the Blur tool (or a combination of both) to carefully erase the lines in the middle.
5. Save your image.

Notes:

_____

_____

_____

_____

_____

_____

_____

_____

_____

_____

Using Hexidecimals To Create A Solid Color Background

Any color that you can create in the RGB color mode can be used as a Web background color. This is done by translating the RGB values for any color or shade into a series of six digits, known as their hexidecimal ("hex") value. The Color Picker has a small box right below the RGB values. This shows the hex value for any color or shade that you choose.

Notes:

_____

_____

_____

_____

_____

_____

_____

_____

_____

_____

_____

_____

_____

Creating a Top Background Border

If you understand that backgrounds are tiles in a Web browser, how hex values work, and how transparency works, you can combine all of these elements to make a simple border with almost no file size weight. Here is an example:

1. Open a file that is 72 pixels wide and 1,440 pixels deep. Make sure you have the rulers turned on.
2. With the square Marquee tool, start from the top and make a box 72 pixels wide and 72 pixels deep.
3. Choose a color from the Color Picker or the Swatches palette, and fill in your box with that color.
4. Repeat 2 and 3 until you reach the bottom.
5. Save the image.

The 1,440 pixel height usually is sufficient to prevent it from repeating. If your page will scroll sufficiently to pass that, simply extend the image to a sufficient length.

Combining Backgrounds and Hexidecimals: Transparency Factors

By making the background color of the image (usually white) transparent, you gain the ability to use the hex color for your background, while retaining the border you designed previously.

Notes:

_____

_____

_____

_____

_____

_____

More Interesting Border Effects

The following are examples of interesting border effects:

• *Creating a Border With Shadows and Ridges*

1. Open a new file, 72 pixels by 1,440 pixels.
2. Add two new layers to your image.
3. Click on Layer 2 to make it the active layer.
4. Use the Square Marquee tool to make a box about 108 pixels wide, and 72 pixels deep.
5. With the Color Picker or the Swatches palette, choose a color you like for your foreground color. Fill the square marquee with this color.
6. Make Layer 1 your active layer by clicking on it.
7. With your square still selected, push the right arrow key three or four times to move your selection on Layer 1 to the right of the selection on Layer 2.
8. Feather your selection by choosing Select → Feather. Feathering makes your edges soft instead of hard.
9. Choose to Feather your selection by 3 pixels and hit OK.
10. Make black your foreground color and fill your selection with it. Play with the opacity slider to select an opacity that gives it a realistic shadow look.
11. Make Layer 2 your active layer again.
12. Add two new layers the same way you did earlier. These new layers will be at the top of the Layers palette. Make Layer 4 the active layer.
13. With the Square Marquee tool, start at the top and make a selection approximately 72 pixels high by 18 pixels wide.
14. Make black your background color. For your foreground color, use the same color that you used to fill your initial selection.
15. Click on the Gradient tool.
16. The available gradient will be, by default, a Foreground to Background gradient. Open the Gradient editor.
17. The gradient bar will show a smooth transition from your foreground color to your background color, with arrows (markers) both above and below the gradient preview bar, at either extreme. The arrows on top represent transparency, while the arrows underneath represent solid color.

18. Click on any of the markers to activate it. Slide the markers along the gradient preview bar to reposition them, and change the overall gradient. If you have activated a Transparency marker (along the top of the bar), you'll have the ability to change the opacity. If you have clicked on a Color marker, you can change the color in that area.

19. You can add color or transparency by clicking anywhere above (transparency) or below (color) the gradient preview bar just by clicking. This will add a new marker. Add one color as close to the middle of the gradient preview bar as you can. Change all the colors of the available markers until the two extreme markers are black, and the center marker is a medium gray.

20. Click OK to go back to your image.

21. With the Gradient tool, start on the left of your marquee selection. Hold the Shift button, to ensure a straight gradient, and pull over to the right of your marquee selection. You will have what looks like a ridge at the top of your image.

22. Put the same ridge at the right of your color field by hitting "v" to select the Move tool. Position your cursor over the ridge and, holding the Option key to access the copy feature and the Shift button to restrict movement, drag downward until you come to the end of your color field.

23. If you like, use Layer 3 to put a shadow under your ridges.

24. Flatten your image and turn change modes to index color. Make the white body of it transparent, and save it as a GIF.

Notes:

_____

_____

_____

_____

_____

_____

• *Ripped, Crinkled Paper Border*

1. Open a new file 216 pixels by 216 pixels.

2. With black and white as your foreground and background colors, respectively, choose Filter → Clouds. Keep hitting Command + F to redo the filter until you get clouds that have a good amount of contrasting areas.

3. Save your file in Photoshop format and name it Clouds.

4. Open a new file, 1,440 pixels by 144 pixels. Create a new layer.

5. Make a square selection at the far left of your new canvas, 144 pixels by 144 pixels. Fill your selection with a light brown/beige color.

6. Choose Filter → Texture → Texturizer. Choose Load Texture and select your file named Clouds. Set the scaling to 100 percent and experiment with the Relief control. The preview window should show your brown plane as having "crinkles" in it. Hit OK.

7. Use the Free-Form lasso tool to select the right edge of the paper jaggedly. Hit Delete.

8. Select the paper edge by first using the Magic Wand tool to select all the white on the right side of your canvas. Press Command + Shift + I (Ctrl + Shift + I in Windows) to select the inverse.

9. Give the edges of your paper a "burnt" look with the Paint Brush tool set to 50% opacity. Click the Wet Edges box in the Options palette and brush along the edge of the crumpled paper border to give it a "burnt" look.

10. Create a rectangular selection around the bottom half of your image.

11. Copy your selection, and paste it back into your image. It will paste back into the area that held your selection but on a new layer.

12. Select Edit → Transform → Flip Vertical. Move the pasted image to the very top, so that the outer edge touches the top and left border of your image.

13. Lightly erase the bottom of the pasted image so that it blends in with the rest of the paper border.

14. Add a drop shadow.

Notes:

SUMMARY

Notes:

_____

_____

_____

_____

_____

_____

_____

_____

_____

_____

_____

_____

_____

_____

Lecture 4 Exercises: Creating Background Graphics and Effects

- Open a new file 200 pixels wide and 200 pixels deep. Use the Pattern Stamp tool to create an image you will use as a background in a Web page. Make sure the image is seamless. Lighten the final image so it's not so distracting on the Web page.
- Open a new file 72 pixels wide and 1440 pixels deep. Create a patterned top border that's 72 pixels deep. Make sure the image is seamless.
- Experiment with creating different background styles with various textures and fills. Play with the edges of a side or top border, as you saw in the ripped, crinkled paper border example.

Lecture Five

Creative Text Effects

Objectives:

- Preview Lecture 5
- Explore Placing Text, the Character Palette, and the Paragraph Palette
- Create Drop Shadows with Layer Attributes
- Add Dimension to Text
- Add Shadows to Text
- Create an Inner Glow, Outer Glow, Bevel, and Emboss
- Explore Issues Associated with New Layer Attributes
- Customize Text Fonts
- Create a Hammered Emboss Effect
- Create Burning and Icy Text
- Create Dotted and Neon Text
- Create 3D and Bubbled Effects
- Fill Part of Your Text with an Image Using Masks
- Review Lecture 5

Placing Text

To place text in your image, activate the Type tool, click on your canvas in the area that you wish to place your text, and start typing. The text will appear on its own layer.

To go back and edit any text that you have placed, activate the Type tool and click any point within your desired copy.

The Character Palette

This palette allows you to establish the font(s) you'll use for your copy, as well as any attributes such as bold, underline, or italics, and font characteristics like the point size of the text, color, and the pixel distance between lines and the letters themselves.

The Paragraph Palette

Allows you to control indentation, right or left justification, and spacing in Text layers.

Notes:

_____

_____

_____

_____

_____

_____

_____

_____

Combine Text And Layer Attributes

Access Layer Attributes by pushing the Layer attributes icon in the Layers menu.

Drop Shadow: Creating Drop Shadows With Layer Attributes

1. Open a new file, 360 pixels wide by 144 pixels high.
2. Select the Type tool and click anywhere on the canvas.
3. Within the Type editor, choose a light color for your text and, using either a bold Helvetica or Arial font, set your font size to 70 points.
4. Type "Web Page" and manually position the words in the middle of the canvas, toward the top.
5. Click OK.
6. Choose Drop Shadow from the Layer attributes.
7. Set your angle to 135 degrees, the distance to 5 pixels, Spread to its default value of 0, and Size to 7.
8. Click OK.

This is one example; change the values above to modify the drop shadow. If you wish to separate the Drop Shadow from the text itself, make sure that the layer named "Web Page" is the active layer, then choose Layer → Layer Style → Create Layer.

Notes:

_____

_____

_____

_____

_____

_____

_____

Adding Dimension to the Text

1. Using the same document, add a layer between the shadow and the text.
2. Press the Command key and click your mouse (Ctrl + click in Windows) on the "Web Page" layer in the Layers palette to get the selection of your text.
3. Press the M key to make the Marquee tool active and use the arrow keys to move your selection down and to the right by two pixels.
4. Fill your selection with black.

Another example:

1. Make the shadow layer active by clicking on it.
2. Choose Edit → Free Transform.
3. Grab one of the bottom corner handles with your cursor and, holding Command and Option (Ctrl + Alt in Windows), drag the corner inward and upward slightly. Get a distance effect by using a feathered, low-opacity eraser over the far end of the shadow.

Notes:

_____

_____

_____

_____

_____

_____

_____

Inner Shadow

1. Type in text.
2. Choose Inner Shadow from the Layer attributes pop-up menu at the bottom of the Layers palette.

This effect works best with sans serif fonts set at a large point size.

Adding Depth to an Inner Shadow

1. Choose Layer → Layer Style → Create Layer to separate the inner shadow into its own layer.
2. Press Command and T (Ctrl + T in Windows) to activate the Free Transform feature.
3. Hold down the Option key (Alt in Windows) and drag one of the corner handles in slightly. Next hold the Command, Option, and Shift keys (Ctrl + Alt + Shift in Windows) to gain control over the perspective, and drag one of the top corner handle bars in slightly. If even more depth is desired, drag the top center handle bar down slightly.

Notes:

_____

_____

_____

_____

_____

_____

_____

_____

Outer Glow

1. Lay out text.
2. Choose Outer Glow from the Layer attributes pop-up menu at the bottom of the Layers palette.

This effect looks the most natural using bright, glowing colors on darker backgrounds.

Inner Glow

1. Type in text.
2. Choose Inner Glow from the Layer attributes pop-up menu at the bottom of the Layers palette.

This effect works best with brighter glows within dark objects.

Notes:

_____

_____

_____

_____

_____

_____

_____

_____

_____

Bevel and Emboss

There are four separate Bevel and Emboss effects: Outer Bevel, Inner Bevel, Emboss, and Pillow Emboss.

- ***Outer Bevel***
  1. Lay out text.
  2. Choose Bevel and Emboss from the Layer attributes pop-up menu.
  3. Choose Outer Bevel from the Style pull-down menu.
  4. Choose settings which produce the bevel effect you want.

- ***Inner Bevel***
  1. Type in text.
  2. Choose Bevel and Emboss.
  3. Choose Inner Bevel.
  4. Choose settings which produce the bevel effect you want.

- ***Emboss***
  1. Type in text.
  2. Choose Bevel and Emboss.
  3. Choose Emboss.
  4. Choose settings which produce the embossed effect you want.

- ***Pillow Emboss***
  1. Type in text.
  2. Choose Bevel and Emboss.
  3. Choose Pillow Emboss.
  4. Choose settings which produce the embossed effect you want.

Notes:

_____

_____

_____

New Layer Attributes in Version 6

Version 6 comes with a few new Layer attributes that weren't available in previous versions of the program.

Satin

This effect gives objects on a layer a satiny look.

Color Overlay and Gradient Overlay

The Color overlay allows you to fill in the objects on your layer with any color and to set your blend mode from the same dialog box. The Gradient overlay does the same thing with a gradient instead of a solid color.

Pattern Overlay

Allows you to choose patterns and scale them to taste.

Stroke

The Stroke Layer attribute gives you complete control over the strokes that you create.

Notes:

_____

_____

_____

_____

_____

_____

_____

_____

Creative Text Design

Creating a Hammered Emboss Effect

1. Open a new file 360 pixels wide by 144 pixels high.
2. Set your foreground to a rich shade of blue and your background color to bright red.
3. Create a diagonal gradient from the top left corner to the bottom right.
4. Choose the Type Mask tool and type "Text Fun" in a Helvetica or Arial font at a point size of 75 points. Click OK and center your text.
5. Choose Select → Feather, and set the Feather radius to 3. Click OK.
6. Choose Select → Save Selection. For Channel, choose New.
7. Choose Filter → Render → Lighting Effects.
8. With the Lighting Style set to Default and the light type set to Spotlight, choose Alpha 1 as your texture channel.
9. Turn the light source so that the spotlight is shining down from a northwest direction. Click OK.

Notes:

_____

_____

_____

_____

_____

_____

_____

Creating Burning, Melting Text

1. Open a new file 360 pixels by 144 pixels.

2. Choose the Type Mask tool and type "TEXT FUN" in all caps, in a Helvetica or Arial font, at a point size of 70 points, and in Bold. Click OK and center your type selection.

3. Create Layer 1.

4. Choose Select → Save Selection and save your selection as an Alpha Channel.

5. Choose Select → Feather and set the Feather radius to 2.

6. Choose a bright red for your foreground color and a medium to dark orange for your background.

7. With the Gradient tool set to Foreground to Background, hold the Shift key down for constraint and drag from the top of your selection to the bottom.

8. Create a new layer over the currently active one.

9. Choose Select → Load Selection.. Make sure that the Channel option is set to the selection you saved earlier.

10. Make your foreground color white. Activate the Airbrush tool.

11. Set the Airbrush opacity to 30. Select a soft brush with a diameter of 100 pixels.

12. Go through the selection so that various parts of your text will appear in a faint white. Deselect your selection when you are through.

13. Choose Filter → Distort → Ocean Ripple. Use the default settings and click OK.

14. Make Layer 1 (your red to orange gradient) your active layer.

15. Choose the Smudge tool, and with a soft brush with a diameter of 27, drag the top of your gradient upward to smear the color. Do this over the top of all your letters. With a smaller brush, make the flame details by smearing the gradient in smaller sections.

16. For a more authentic flame, try adding some yellow to the middle of your red to orange gradient.

Another technique for this effect:

1. Open a new file 360 pixels wide by 360 pixels deep.
2. Fill the background with black.
3. Use the Type tool to place the word "TEXT" in the center of the canvas. Use white for the letters.
4. Flatten your image and choose Image → Rotate Canvas → 90° CW.
5. Choose Filter → Stylize → Wind. Choose Wind for the method and From the Left for the direction. Click OK.
6. Hit Command and F (Ctrl + F in Windows) twice to exaggerate the effect of the filter.
7. Rotate your canvas 90° CCW.
8. Select Filter → Blur → Motion Blur. Set the angle to 59° with a blur of 4 pixels and click OK.
9. Choose Filter → Distort → Ripple and maintain the default settings. Click OK.
10. Add a new layer and fill it with a bright yellow. Change the layer mode to Overlay. Add another layer and fill it with bright red. Also change this layer's mode to Overlay.

Notes:

_____

_____

_____

_____

_____

_____

Creating Icy Letters

1. Open a new file 360 pixels wide by 360 pixels deep.
2. Fill the background with black.
3. Use the Type tool to place the word "TEXT" in the center of the canvas. Choose an icy sky blue color for the letters.
4. Flatten your image, and choose Image → Rotate Canvas → 90° CW.
5. Choose Filter → Stylize → Wind. Choose Wind for the method and From the Right for the direction. Click OK.
6. Press Command and F (Ctrl + F in Windows) two or three more times until your icicles are as long as you'd like them.
7. Rotate your canvas 90° CCW.
8. Choose Filter → Brush Strokes → Accented Edges. Set the Edge width to 2, the Edge brightness to 38, and Smoothness to 5.
9. Create a new layer, and with the Airbrush tool brush randomly over the text; make sure that you have white as your foreground color, and choose a brush size of around 35 pixels. When finished, set the Layer mode to Overlay.

Notes:

_____

_____

_____

_____

_____

_____

_____

Creating Dotted Text

1. Open a new file 504 pixels wide by 144 pixels deep.
2. With the Type Mask tool, place the words "TEXT FUN" in the center of your canvas.
3. Choose Select → Feather and set the Feather radius to 4.
4. Deselect all.
5. Choose Filter → Pixelate → Color Halftone. Lower the maximum radius to 4 and click OK.

Notes:

_____

_____

_____

_____

_____

_____

_____

_____

_____

_____

_____

_____

Creating Neon Text

1. Open a new file 504 pixels wide by 144 pixels deep.
2. Use the Type Mask tool to write "TEXT FUN."
3. Choose Select → Feather and set the Feather radius to 3.
4. Fill your selection with black. Deselect all.
5. With black and white as your foreground and background colors, choose Filter → Render → Difference Clouds.
6. Choose Image → Adjust → Invert.
7. Overlay any color.

Notes:

_____

_____

_____

_____

_____

_____

_____

_____

_____

_____

_____

_____

Creating Quick 3D Text

1. Open a new file 576 pixels wide by 144 pixels deep.

2. With the Type tool, type "TEXT FUN" and center it on your canvas.

3. Choose Layer → Rasterize→ Type. This will turn your text into a regular graphic.

4. Choose Edit → Free Transform.

5. Grab the bottom right corner handle and, while pressing the Shift, Option and Command buttons (Shift + Alt + Ctrl in Windows), drag outward. Drag one of the top corner handles and drag inward. Hit Return (Enter in Windows) or double-click on the text.

6. In the Layers palette options menu, select Duplicate Layer. Accept the default setting; the new layer will appear just above your original. Make the previous layer the active layer.

7. Choose Filter → Blur → Motion Blur. Set your angle to 90° and your distance to 75.

8. With your Move tool, move the blur down until it fits below your letters.

Notes:

_____

_____

_____

_____

_____

_____

_____

Creating Bubbled Text

1. Open a new file 576 pixels wide by 144 pixels deep.
2. With the Type tool, type "TEXT FUN" and center it on your canvas.
3. Choose Layer → Type → Render Layer.
4. Select the letters by pressing Command and clicking (Ctrl + clicking in Windows) on the text layer in the Layer palette. Save your selection as a channel.
5. Deselect all and choose Filter → Render → 3D Transform.
6. Using the sphere tool, create a sphere around part of the letters. Use the trackball tool and rotate the sphere upward just a bit.
7. Erase the bottom of the sphere.
8. Create a new layer in between the background and your text layer. Load the Alpha Channel you created earlier.
9. Choose Select → Feather and feather your image by 4 pixels. Fill it with black.
10. Lower the opacity on your layer to around 30% and move your shadow a little off center.

Notes:

_____

_____

_____

_____

_____

_____

_____

_____

Filling Part of Your Text With an Image (Working With Masks)

1. Open a new file 576 pixels wide by 144 pixels deep.
2. With the Type tool, type "TEXT FUN" and center it on your canvas.
3. Choose Layer → Type → Render Layer.
4. Press Command and click (Ctrl + click in Windows) the text layer to grab the selection and save the selection as a channel.
5. In the Channels palette click on the channel.
6. With the Gradient tool, hold the Shift key for constraint and make a gradient from top to bottom, white to black.
7. Choose Select → Load Selection, and choose your channel. Click on the channel marked RGB to load the selection into the color channel.
8. Open an image on a separate canvas. Copy the image to your pasteboard.
9. Back in your original canvas, the top of your text is still selected. Use the Paste Into command to paste your image into your selection.

Notes:

_____

_____

_____

_____

_____

_____

_____

_____

_____

SUMMARY

Notes:

_____

_____

_____

_____

_____

_____

_____

_____

_____

_____

_____

_____

_____

_____

_____

_____

_____

Lecture 5 Exercises: Creative Text Effects

1. Open the file EX1_3.JPG from your Lecture 1 exercises. Select the text layer containing the text "Sunset in Boston." Apply a burning effect to this text using the second technique presented in this lecture. Save your work as EX5_1.JPG.

2. Open a new file 638 pixels wide and 410 pixels deep. Type the word BOSTON in all capital letters, Helvetica Bold, 125-point type. Apply a bulge effect to the text. Open the file BOSTON.JPG in a separate canvas and fill the text BOSTON with the image. Save your work as EX5_2.JPG.

3. Open a new file 500 pixels wide by 150 pixels deep. Type the words Photoshop 6. Practice applying various effects to this text, including the following:
   • Icing Effect
   • Hammered Embossed Effect
   • Neon Effect

Lecture Six

Navigation, Buttons, and Bullets

Objectives:

- Preview Lecture 6

- Explore Issues Associated with Navigation

- Create Beveled Buttons Using Several Techniques

- Create Circular Bevels

- Create Buttons with Brushed Metal Texture

- Create Water Puddle Buttons

- Review Lecture 6

The Importance of Navigation

Keep the following points in mind when developing the navigation for a site:

- The only reliable places to put navigation elements are either along the top or down the left side.
- Keep the primary navigational elements (the buttons that lead from the home page to the pages one tier down) visible at all times.
- Secondary and tertiary navigation should be visible and placed in a standard, consistent location.
- Create your site so that any one page can be accessed from any other pages with three or four clicks.
- Keep button names short and to the point.
- It helps to lay out the hierarchy of a site on paper before you start to build the site.

All of the following examples use button sizes which are very large; they can always be reduced when needed.

Notes:

_____

_____

_____

_____

_____

_____

_____

_____

Creating Beveled Buttons

Using Simple Bevels to Create Buttons

1. Open a new file, 216 pixels by 72 pixels.
2. Create Layer 1 and make that the active layer.
3. Choose a light shade of blue to fill your canvas.
4. Choose Bevel and Emboss from the Layer palette.
5. Choose Inner Bevel for the Style.
6. Set Angle to 120°, Depth to the maximum 20 pixels, and Blur to 10.

Notes:

_____

_____

_____

_____

_____

_____

_____

_____

_____

_____

_____

Creating Buttons With Dual Bevel

1. Use the Rectangular Marquee tool to make a selection of the solid blue area in your button.
2. Choose Select → Modify → Contract and choose a setting of 3.
3. Press Command and C (Ctrl + C in Windows) to copy your selection, and then Command + V (Ctrl + V in Windows) to paste it in the same spot but on a new layer.
4. Choose Layer → Attributes → Bevel and Emboss and, keeping the angle and the depth the same, push the Radio button for down instead of up, and lower the blur to 2.

Notes:

_____

_____

_____

_____

_____

_____

_____

_____

_____

_____

_____

_____

Using Traditional Methods for Bevels

1. Open a new file 216 pixels by 72 pixels.
2. Choose a color to fill your canvas.
3. Select All, choose Select → Modify → Border, and choose a border setting of 12.
4. Choose Select → Save Selection, and choose New in the Channel pull-down menu.
5. Deselect all and choose Filter → Render → Lighting Effects. In the Texture channel pull-down menu, select Alpha 1. Set the direction of your light. Click OK.

Creating Traditional Dual Bevel

1. Working from the previous example, open the Channels palette. Make Alpha 1 the active channel. Select All by pressing Command and A (Ctrl + A in Windows). Choose Select → Modify → border and set the border to 24.
2. Choose Select → Save Selection. This time your new channel is automatically named Alpha 2. Make Alpha 2 the active layer.
3. Press Command and L (Ctrl + L in Windows). Increase the highlights in Input Levels to 195. Set the Midtones slider to 0.85.
4. Deselect all.
5. Click the RGB channel.
6. Go to the Lighting Effects filter and adjust the lighting to fit your preference. Click OK.

Notes:

_____

_____

_____

_____

_____

Creating Circular Bevels

Creating A Simple Circular Bevel

1. Open a new file, 216 pixels by 216 pixels.
2. Create a new layer.
3. Using the Elliptical Marquee tool, hold down the Shift key for constraint and drag to create a circle in the middle of the canvas.
4. Set the background color to black and choose some light shade of blue for your foreground color. Using the Gradient tool, with the options set to Foreground to Background, drag a gradient from the northwest position of your circle to the southeast position.
5. Press Command and C (Ctrl + C in Windows) to copy the circle to your clipboard. Press Command and V (Ctrl + V in Windows) to paste it back again.
6. Choose Edit → Transform → Rotate 180°.
7. Choose Edit → Transform → Numeric Transform. Make sure that Scale is checked, and reduce your selection to 80% on both axes.
8. Add a shadow to the button by making Layer 1 the active layer again, and choose Drop Shadow from the Layers attributes icon; select a distance of 10 and a blur of 20.

Notes:

_____

_____

_____

_____

_____

_____

_____

_____

Creating a Pushed-in "Coat" Button

1. Follow Steps 1–3 from "Creating a Simple Circular Bevel."
2. Fill your selection with a light shade of blue.
3. Choose Select → Save Selection, and save your selection as Alpha 1.
4. Make Alpha 1 your active channel.
5. Establish a middle point on the circle.
6. With the Radial Gradient tool selected, and the gradient range set to Foreground to Background, drag a gradient from your center point to the edge of your circle.
7. Press Command and L (Ctrl + L in Windows). Set the Shadows level to 32, and the highlights level to 235.
8. Make the RGB channel active again.
9. Choose Filter → Render → Lighting Effects. Set your light type to Spotlight and move the direction to coming from the northwest. Make sure that the White high option is clicked, and set your Texture channel to Alpha 1.

Notes:

_____

_____

_____

_____

_____

_____

_____

_____

Creating a Pill-Shaped Button: Photoshop 5.5 and Lower

1. Open a new file, 432 pixels by 216 pixels.

2. Open a new layer and, using the Elliptical Marquee tool, hold the Shift key down and make a circle toward the left side of your canvas.

3. Select the Paintbucket tool and fill your circle with a light shade of blue.

4. Select your Move tool and, holding the Option and Shift (Alt + Shift in Windows) keys down, drag a copy of the circle to the other side of the canvas.

5. Pinpoint the center diameter of both circles.

6. Select View → Snap to Guides to make sure that your next selection will hug the rules you just made.

7. With the Rectangular Marquee tool, make a selection from the top left corner of your rules to the bottom right corner. Fill your new selection with the same color that you used to fill the circles.

8. Select your entire image. Start a new layer so that you don't disturb the pill you just created.

9. Choose Reflected gradient as your tool and press the D and X keys. Starting from the middle of your selection, drag a gradient downward and just slightly to the right to create a diagonal gradient.

10. In the Layers palette, select "soft light" for your mode.

11. Choose Bevel and Emboss.

12. Select Emboss as your style.

Notes:

_____

_____

_____

_____

_____

Creating Buttons with Texture Added

Creating Buttons With a Brushed Metal Texture

The brushed metal effect comes out well if you create the texture at 150–200 ppi and then scale it down.

1. Open a new file, 432 pixels by 216 pixels, 200 ppi.
2. Create a new layer.
3. Make white your background color and a medium to dark gray your foreground color.
4. Make the Gradient tool active. From the Options palette, click on the Gradient preview to access the Gradient editor.
5. Create a gradient by alternating between the foreground color and the background color to simulate stripes.
6. Drag the Gradient tool crosshairs from the top left corner to set your gradient.
7. Your canvas should look as though there is light reflecting off it.
8. Choose Filter → Noise → Add Noise. Set the noise Amount to 50, using a uniform distribution.
9. Choose Filter → Blur → Motion Blur. Set the angle to match the direction that your light hits are going. Set Blur Distance to 110.
10. Choose Image → Adjust → Color Balance. In the midtones, move the top slider closer to Cyan until the first numeric color level reads –16. Move the bottom slider closer to Blue until the last number color level reads +28.
11. Select Image → Image Size and reduce your image to 72 ppi.
12. Bevel the button with one of the methods described earlier.
13. Using the Type Mask tool, open the text editor and type "HOME" in large letters.
14. Move your text selection where you want it and push Command and C (Ctrl + C in Windows) to copy that part of the image to the pasteboard. Now press Command and V (Ctrl + V in Windows) to paste it back.
15. Open the Bevel and Emboss dialog box and choose appropriate settings.

Notes:

Creating Water Puddle Buttons

1. Open a new file, 600 pixels by 400 pixels, 200 ppi.
2. Create a new layer.
3. Use your Free Form lasso tool to make a wavy, elliptical selection.
4. Make white your foreground color and select a light shade of blue for your background color.
5. Create a Radial Gradient from white to light blue.
6. Deselect your selection.
7. Open the Bevel and Emboss dialog box; choose Inner Bevel.
8. Set Depth to 10 pixels, and Blur to 20 pixels.
9. Choose Filter → Distort → Zig Zag. Set Amount to 34% and Ridges to 7%.
10. Opening the Bevel and Emboss dialog box; set Opacity to 40%, Distance to 3, and Blur to 4.
11. Place the button name on your puddle.
12. Choose Layer → Type → Render Layer.
13. Select Filter → Distort → Ripple; set Ripple amount to 115% and Size to Medium.

Notes:

_____

_____

_____

_____

_____

_____

_____

SUMMARY

Notes:

_____

_____

_____

_____

_____

_____

_____

_____

_____

_____

_____

_____

_____

_____

_____

_____

Lecture 6 Exercises: Navigation, Buttons, and Bullets

11. Create a pill-shaped button with an inner ridge that contains the puddle effect that you saw applied to the Home button in the lecture.

12. Open each one of the following files:
    - SAX.JPG
    - PIANOKEYS.JPG
    - GUITAR.JPG
    - BRASS.JPG
    - VIOLINS.JPG

Create a new button for each of these graphics, sized at about 125 pixels wide and 81 pixels high. You will have to rotate some of these images so they are all the same orientation. Practice using some of the bevel and other effects you learned in this lecture. Supply a textual description for each and apply textual effects as well.

13. Using the same graphic files from the preceding Exercise, create a button-oriented navigation bar that would be used at a Web site, much like the one you saw in the Novartis IT Virtual Office example in this lecture. Save this navigation bar as EX6_3.JPG.

Lecture Seven

Inline Graphics

Objectives:

- Preview Lecture 7
- Scanning Photos into Photoshop
- Explore Other Ways to Get Images into Photoshop
- Resize and Resample Images
- Crop Image Edges
- Remove Dust and Scratches
- Remove Noise from an Image
- Sharpen Blurred Photographs
- Use Color Correction Tools
- Create Cool Lightning Effects
- Create Cool Collage Effects
- Turn a 2D Image into a 3D Image
- Create the Illusion of Speed
- Create Drop Shadow Frames and Curved Corners
- Use Filters to Create Borders
- Create "Spirograph" and Tie-Die Frames
- Use Third-Party Filters for Image Effects
- Review Lecture 7

Getting Images into Photoshop

There are several ways to get images into Photoshop.

Personal Scanners

You will first have to install the proper drivers and software to use a personal scanner. Having done so, the documentation for that scanner should tell you which Import options to use for scanning material into Photoshop. Note that since Web graphics have a maximum resolution of 72 ppi, you can usually set the scanner to that resolution if your only intended use for the image is for Web display.

Photo CD-ROMs

Advantages of getting your pictures put on a Photo CD:

1. You don't have to do your own scanning.
2. A small additional price per image will give you a number of resolutions.
3. The CD will act as storage so you can use a minimal amount of hard drive space.
4. Printed icons of the images on the back of the CD case will help catalog your images for future use.

Stock Photo CDs

Stock images are usually sold in one of two ways:

- You can purchase one CD that contains multiple images, any of which you have the right to use.
- You can choose a picture or set of pictures from a catalog or CD sampler and negotiate a price with the stock house.

Low-res images can also be downloaded directly from the Web.

Digital Cameras

These produce instant images on demand, and are already in computer-ready format.

Notes:

Resizing and Resampling Images

Resizing implies changing the physical/display size of the image without changing the number of pixels.

Resampling involves changing the number of pixels and thus adjusting the image accordingly. It is rarely useful when increasing size, but sometimes very useful when reducing size.

Both are accessed through the Image → Image Size menu choice.

When resampling, you have three choices for the method used:

- *Bicubic* is the smoothest, but also the slowest.
- *Bilinear* is faster.
- *Nearest Neighbor* duplicates or throws away pixels as needed.

Notes:

_____

_____

_____

_____

_____

_____

_____

_____

_____

_____

Photo Retouching Techniques

Cropping Image Edges

There are several reasons to use cropping, ranging from bad initial scanning to reducing file size.

1. **Using the Crop Tool**
   1. Choose the Crop tool from the toolbar.
   2. Drag a selection around the portion of your image that you wish to keep.
   3. Drag your mouse in the direction of either arrow to crop at the appropriate angle. To change the center of rotation, drag the point of origin (the center crosshair in the crop marquee) to another area of the image.
   4. Press the Return/Enter button to crop your selection, or the Esc button to cancel your selection.

2. **Using the Marquee to Crop**
   1. Use the Rectangular marquee to make a selection around the area you wish to keep.
   2. Choose Image → Crop.

3. **Changing the Canvas Size to Crop an Image**
   1. Decide the portion of your image that you wish to delete.
   2. Choose Image → Canvas Size. Reduce the width and height by the amount that was measured out in Step 1.
   3. The Anchor point in the dialog box represents the full image in nine separate squares. Choose the anchor box that best fits your selection.
   4. Click Proceed.

4. **Cropping to Make Sizes Match**
   1. Copy and paste one image into the canvas of another.
   2. Choose Edit → Free Transform, and drag one of the corner handlebars in or out until the posted image is the desired size.

Notes:

Removing Dust and Scratches

There are a number of different ways that you can get rid of dust, scratches, and even rips in your photographs when working in Photoshop. Here are a couple:

- For photos with a significant number of specks, dots, and dust, use the Dust & Scratches filter by choosing Filter → Noise → Dust & Scratches.
- For just a few specks and dust particles, zoom in by 2 or 3X, select a part of the image that has a similar tone or pattern, and clone it with a soft-edged, small brush over the dusty/scratched areas.

Notes:

_____

_____

_____

_____

_____

_____

_____

_____

_____

_____

Removing Noise From an Image

Here are a few of the more popular and effective techniques:

- ***Using the Despeckle Filter***

  Choose Filter → Noise → Despeckle to activate this tool.

- ***Using the Median Filter***

  Choose Filter → Noise → Median. The greater the radius value, the more severe the final effect will be on your image.

- ***Using the Gaussian Blur Filter***

  Choose Filter → Blur → Gaussian Blur. The higher the blur radius, the more severe the effect it will have on your image.

Notes:

_____

_____

_____

_____

_____

_____

_____

_____

_____

_____

_____

Sharpening Blurred Photographs

There are effective ways to sharpen a blurred photograph. Within the Filter → Sharpen submenu, there are four filters: Sharpen, Sharpen Edges, Sharpen More, and Unsharp Mask. The most powerful of them is the latter. It has three control values:

- Amount determines the percentage (from 1-500) of sharpening. The higher the percentage, the more severe the sharpen effect.
- The Radius slider sets the thickness of the edges that are sharpened.
- Setting the level of the Threshold determines the difference between the target pixel and its neighboring pixels that must exist before Photoshop sharpens those pixels. Lower threshold = greater effect.

Because it has these three separate control values, Unsharp Mask can be difficult to master.

Notes:

_____

_____

_____

_____

_____

_____

_____

_____

_____

Color Correction Tools and Techniques

There are several color correction tools and techniques.
For adjusting a flat-looking scan or picture:

- Image → Adjust → Levels has three control values. The left slider adjusts the shadows, the middle slider adjusts the midtones, and the right slider adjusts the highlights.
- Image → Adjust → Curves displays a full tonal range graph of your image Curves which will let you make adjustments at any point along the 255-point range.

To add color to a picture that seems washed-out:
Select the area you want to adjust, and:

5. Choose Image → Adjust → Color Balance. This allows you to add colors to and simultaneously subtract colors from the image for any of three tonal ranges: shadows, midtones, and highlights. And/Or,
6. In the Color Picker, select the new color you want for the selection. Add a new layer and, with the selection still active, fill the selection with the chosen color. In the Mode pull-down menu on the front of the Layers palette, choose Overlay, combining the chosen color with the underlying image, increasing the color intensity without losing the details of the original.

Notes:

_____

_____

_____

_____

_____

_____

Adjusting Color With Hue/Saturation

Image → Adjust → Hue/Saturation lets you change the color as well as its saturation and light/darkness. Use the top slider (Hue) to change the color completely, the center slider (Saturation) to add or subtract richness from the color, and the bottom slider (Lightness) to add highlights or shadows.

Notes:

_____

_____

_____

_____

_____

_____

_____

_____

_____

_____

_____

_____

Cool Lightning Effects

Below are two methods to create lightning:

TECHNIQUE 1:

1. Open a new file, 360 by 360 pixels, with a black background.
2. Create two new layers immediately, and make sure Layer 2 is your active layer.
3. Use white as your foreground color and make your Paintbrush the active tool.
4. Choose a brush that is 4 pixels in diameter with a soft edge. Begin drawing a jagged line from the top of your canvas toward the bottom, creating the main current in what will be an electrical storm. Use a smaller brush, 2 pixels in diameter, to create the "arms" of your current.
5. Choose one with a diameter of 1. These will be the faintest currents.
6. Once you have your lightning bolts where you want them, make Layer 1 your active layer. Hold the Command button (Ctrl in Windows) while clicking Layer 2 in the Layers palette to select your lightning.
7. Choose Select → Modify → Expand and expand all the pixels by 1.
8. Choose Select → Feather and set the radius to 1.
9. Fill your selection with a bright yellow. Lower the layer opacity to 50%.
10. As a final touch, we'll put a light flash where the lightning may have struck. In the Layers palette, choose New Layer (instead of clicking the New Layer icon at the bottom of the palette).
11. Under the Mode pull-down menu, choose Screen and deselect the box Fill with screen neutral black.
12. With the Circle marquee tool, make a circle around the bottom of your main current and Feather it with a radius of 4.
13. Choose Filter → Render → Lens Flare. Set the Flare to 155, directly centered, and click OK.
14. Use the Move tool to move your flare around if necessary.

TECHNIQUE 2:

1. Open a new file 360 by 360 pixels.
2. Make sure that your background and foreground colors are set to black and white, respectively.
3. Create a gradient from the top left corner to the bottom right.
4. Choose Filter → Render → Difference Clouds to fill your canvas with a cloud texture; redo the filter until you get clouds with high contrasts.
5. Press Command and I (Ctrl + I in Windows) to invert the colors.
6. Open the Levels dialog box, and pull the Shadow arrow over until the background gets darker and the lightning becomes the focal point of your canvas.
7. On a new layer, fill the canvas with a dark blue. Set the Color mode to Soft Light.

Notes:

_____

_____

_____

_____

_____

_____

_____

_____

_____

_____

Creating Cool Collage Effects

1. Open two photographs to make your collage.

2. With the Marquee tool, make a selection around a portion of the main subject in Picture One and copy the selection to your pasteboard.

3. Deselect your selection.

4. Paste the image from your clipboard back into Picture One.

5. Choose Edit → Free Transform and manipulate the size by dragging one of the corner handles outward until the image is nearly three times its original size.

6. Drag the Opacity slider on the Layers palette down to 40%.

7. Access the Levels dialog box. Manipulate Input Highlights by dragging the slider on the right out to the left, until you begin to lose tone and detail in the image. Do the same with the Output Highlights slider.

8. Make the background layer active.

9. Choose the Move tool, and drag the entire image in Picture Two onto the canvas in Picture One.

10. Create a mask of your image on Layer 2 by dragging Layer 2 down to the Create Mask icon at the bottom of the Layers palette (the first icon on the left).

11. Activate the Linear Gradient tool. Create a gradient from black to white, left to right over the entire image in Layer 2. Hold the Shift key down to ensure that your gradient stays straight and is not made at an angle.

12. Reduce the Layer 2 opacity to 15% so that your image is more subtle.

13. Erase portions of your image on all layers so that your image looks complete without hard edges.

14. Choose Image → Image Size and change your resolution from 200 to 72 ppi.

Other Collage Tips: Defringing and Removing Mattes

If you experience haloing, choose Layer $\rightarrow$ Matting $\rightarrow$ Defringe and choose a width that will be wide enough to remove the halo. If your halo came from a white or a black background, choose Remove White Matte or Remove Black Matte, respectively.

Notes:

_____

_____

_____

_____

_____

_____

_____

_____

_____

_____

_____

_____

_____

_____

_____

_____

Turning a 2D Image Into a 3D Image

1. Open or create a 2D image.
2. Choose Filter → Render → 3D Transform.
3. Choose the cube.
4. In the preview window, drag from the top left corner to the bottom right corner of your image.
5. Use the Direct Selection tool (the white arrow in the upper right of the toolbar) and drag the lower right handle on the wireframe to the bottom right corner of your image. Drag the lower center handle to the bottom left corner of your image.
6. Click on the Trackball tool and drag your selection to the right and downward so that your image displays three sides.
7. Click OK.
8. The 3D image is directly above the original 2D image and on the same layer. Use a selection technique to grab the 3D box (try the Polygon lasso, clicking on all corners of your 3D image). Cut and paste, then dispose of the layer containing the original image.

Notes:

_____

_____

_____

_____

_____

_____

_____

_____

Creating the Illusion of Speed

1. Open a picture of something which would be expected to move fast. Make sure that the subject of your image is on its own layer—not the background layer.

2. Move your main subject to one of the sides of your canvas.

3. Copy your image and paste it so that your copy appears on a new, higher layer, lined up horizontally with the original image.

4. Lower the opacity of the layer containing the original image to around 50%.

5. Choose Filter → Blur → Motion Blur and set the angle to 0°. Move the distance slider to the right until you get the motion distance that you like.

Notes:

_____

_____

_____

_____

_____

_____

_____

_____

_____

_____

_____

_____

Methods for Framing Images

Drop Shadows

1. Select all of your image.
2. Copy and paste the image to a new layer.
3. If necessary, increase the size of the canvas, keeping your image in the upper left.
4. Choose Layers → Effects → Drop Shadow and play with the settings.

Notes:

_____

_____

_____

_____

_____

_____

_____

_____

_____

_____

_____

_____

_____

Curved Corners

1. Create a shape with rounded corners on its own layer.
2. Create a marquee selection of the shape.
3. Create a new layer and stroke the selection by choosing Edit → Stroke and set Stroke Width and Location to the desired settings.
4. Paste the image you want to frame into the stroked selection.

Notes:

_____

_____

_____

_____

_____

_____

_____

_____

_____

_____

_____

_____

_____

Using Filters to Create Picture Borders

• *Mosaic Tile Border*

1. Select all of your image.
2. Choose Select → Modify → Border and set the border width to 20.
3. Select Filter → Texture → Mosaic Tile.

• *Cloud Border*

1. Select all of your image.
2. Set the border width to 20.
3. Select Filter → Render → Clouds.

• *Polka Dot Border*

1. Select all of your image.
2. Set the border width to 20.
3. Select Filter → Pixelate → Color Halftone.

• *Brick Border*

1. Select all of your image
2. Set the border width to 20
3. Select Filter → Texturizer and choose Brick texture.

Notes:

_____

_____

_____

_____

_____

"Spirograph" Frame

1. On a layer directly over the image you want to frame, choose a regular Square Marquee selection.
2. Stroke the selection to create a border.
3. Create a new layer above the one on which you are working.
4. Create a smaller Square Marquee selection inside the original one.
5. Make sure that everything is deselected, and choose Filter → Blur → Radial Blur; set the amount to 15.
6. Open the Levels dialog box, and increase the shadows.
7. Complete Steps 5 and 6 for both borders.

Notes:

_____

_____

_____

_____

_____

_____

_____

_____

_____

_____

_____

_____

The Tie-Dye Ring

1. On a new layer above the image that you want to frame, create a Marquee circle selection, then choose Select → Inverse.

2. With the Radial Gradient tool, set a gradient from white to black.

3. Choose Filter → Pixelate → Color Halftone.

4. Choose Filter → Distort → Twirl and set the Angle value to 999°.

5. Create one more circle selections outside where the color was affected by the Twirl filter, inverse the selection, and delete the contents.

6. Create a drop shadow using Layer Attributes to add some depth.

Notes:

_____

_____

_____

_____

_____

_____

_____

_____

_____

_____

_____

_____

SUMMARY

Notes:

_____

_____

_____

_____

_____

_____

_____

_____

_____

_____

_____

_____

_____

_____

_____

_____

_____

_____

Lecture 7 Exercises: Inline Graphics: Image is Everything

- Open the file OLDPHOTO.JPG. As you can see, this is a scan of an old photograph, one that is of questionable quality and is torn and wrinkled in several spots. Using the tools you learned about in this lecture, restore this image in the best way you can.
- Create a collage like the one presented in this lecture using the following files:
  - SAX.JPG
  - PIANOKEYS.JPG
  - GUITAR.JPG
  - BRASS.JPG
  - VIOLINS.JPG
  - MUSICNOTES.JPG

  Use MUSICNOTES.JPG as your background. Save the finished file as EX7_2.JPG.
- Open the file TALLSHIP.JPG. Change the sky in this image so that it appears overcast. Add lightning to create a dramatic effect.
- Practice creating special effects starting from nothing, such as you saw in the water droplets example in this lecture. Use filters and layer effects to complete this Exercise.

Lecture Eight

ImageReady: Springboard to the Web

Objectives:

- Preview Lecture 8

- Explore ImageReady and Photoshop Working Together

- Optimize Images

- Create, Play, and Stop Animations

- Change the Speed and Frame Order of Your Animation

- Create Tweening Frames

- Mix Animation and Transparency

- Save, Open, and Optimize an ImageReady Animation

- Create Slices in Your ImageReady Images

- Select and Optimize Slices

- Turn an Auto-Slice Into a User-Slice

- Resize and Move a Slice

- Divide, Combine, and Align Slices

- Use the Slice Palette

- Save Image Slices

- Add a Drop Shadow Rollover

- Explore Issues Associated with Rollovers

- Create a Rollover Change Elsewhere in Your Image and Trigger an Animation as a State

- Review Lecture 8

ImageReady and Photoshop: How They Differ, How They Work Together

Photoshop is best used for the major work on images – creation, manipulation, retouching, and so on. ImageReady's main function is to help create the special Web effects that Photoshop simply wasn't designed to do: creating slices, animations, and rollovers for your Web site.

Quantum Leap: Jumping Between Programs

The Jump To button gives you easy access to either program, with virtually no hassles. To use the button, simply press it. It is even possible to add other programs into the "Jump To" menu.

When you jump to ImageReady from Photoshop (and back again), the image you are working in will open in the other program. If you have made changes since your last jump, you will be notified and asked if you want to update it before making the jump.

Notes:

_____

_____

_____

_____

_____

_____

_____

_____

_____

Interface Differences

The Save for Web function in Photoshop 6 allows you to view your image as you tweak the settings in one of four ways. In ImageReady you don't need to choose Save for Web for these options; they're built-in to the main ImageReady interface.

The Drawback of Working in 2-Up or 4-Up

There is one potential problem associated with working in the 2-Up or 4-Up views: The images in all preview windows have to update after each and every change you make. Since this requires processing time for each preview, even a fast computer can show a noticeable delay after each change, interrupting your workflow. This can be switched off by de-selecting Auto-Regenerate from the Optimize palette's pull-down menu. Of course, this means that you will have to force manual regeneration (through the Warning icon or the Optimize menu) whenever you want to view the updated versions of the preview windows.

Notes:

_____

_____

_____

_____

_____

_____

_____

_____

Layers and Layer Options

ImageReady's Layers palette differs from Photoshop's in the addition of the Fast Forward and Rewind buttons, and in how the palette and programs deal with Layer effects.

Layer Effects

All of the Layer effects in ImageReady have their own palettes, rather than using a dialogue box as in Photoshop.

Creating Styles (ImageReady)

Styles are rather like packaged Actions. To create a Style:

1. In your Layers palette create a Layer effect or series of effects.
2. Select one of the effects by clicking on it, or select all of the effects in a group by clicking the Style icon.
3. Open the Styles palette by choosing Window → Show Styles.
4. Drag the effect or set of effects to the Styles palette.

Styles can also retain rollover states.

Notes:

_____

_____

_____

_____

_____

_____

_____

_____

Making Selections

Some of the more advanced selection methods, such as Extract, Background eraser, and Quick Masks, don't exist in ImageReady. However, ImageReady provides the Rounded Rectangular marquee tool, which lets you make rectangular selections with curved corners.

The History Palette

In ImageReady, the History palette provides a visible list of the commands you have made. Neither the History brush nor the Art History brush is available.

Notes:

_____

_____

_____

_____

_____

_____

_____

_____

_____

_____

_____

_____

Optimizing Images

The options provided in Photoshop are also found in ImageReady in a separate palette rather than via a dialogue box. Optimization can be set while you are working on an image.

Notes:

_____

_____

_____

_____

_____

_____

_____

_____

_____

_____

_____

_____

_____

Creating Animations

In ImageReady, animations are done with the Animation palette. A simple "bouncing ball" example demonstrates its use:

1. In Photoshop, create a new file, 72 x 216 pixels and immediately create two new layers. Begin working on Layer 2.
2. With your Circular Shape tool, hold the Shift key for constraint and make a circle toward the bottom of your canvas.
3. Create a new layer and change your foreground color to black. Within the circular selection, use your airbrush to put a shadow on the bottom and a small highlight on the top.
4. From the Layers palette, choose Merge down. Rename the layer "Ball 1."
5. On Layer 1, use your Elliptical Marquee tool to make an oval beneath your red ball. Choose Select → Feather with a feather radius of 5 to soften the edges. Click OK.
6. Fill the selection with black to create a shadow. Rename the layer "Shadow."
7. Reactivate the "Ball 1" layer, and choose Duplicate Layer from the palette pull-down menu. Name the new, duplicated layer "Ball 2" and click OK. Do this three times for a total of four separate balls.
8. On each duplicated layer, move the ball upward with the Move tool. Hold down Shift key while moving.

To make the ball actually "bounce," we will create the animation sequence in ImageReady.

1. As a note, always do the bulk of image work in Photoshop, as we did above.
2. Open your canvas in ImageReady by clicking the Jump To button.
3. Open the Animation palette by choosing Window → Show Animation.
4. Notice that the preview shown looks exactly like your main canvas, since all the layers are visible.
5. Turn off Ball 2, 3, and 4 layers by clicking the Eye icon at the far left of each of those layers.

6. Create a new animation frame either by clicking on the New Frame icon at the bottom of the Animation palette or by choosing New Frame from the Animation palette menu.

7. Hide the Frame 1 layer.

8. Make the Ball 2 layer visible by clicking the empty box on the far left of the layer in the Layers palette. Also, make the Shadow layer active by clicking on it. Change Opacity to 66% in the Layers palette.

9. To see how these changes are affecting only the active animation frame, make Frame 1 active by clicking on it. Click back to Frame 2 to see the changes in the Layers palette again.

10. Create a new frame in the Animation palette.

11. Hide the Ball 2 layer and make the Ball 3 layer visible. Also, with the Shadow layer active, reduce the shadow opacity to 33%.

12. Create a new frame.

13. Hide Ball 3 and make Ball 4 visible. Also, reduce the opacity of the Shadow layer to 1%.

14. Now that the ball is as high as it can go, do the whole thing in reverse. Leave out the uppermost and lowermost states on the way down.

Notes:

_____

_____

_____

_____

_____

_____

_____

Miscellaneous Animation Points

- You didn't necessarily have to create the layers in Photoshop. You can also create layers in ImageReady.
- If you alter a layer, the changes only appear in those frames which actually display that layer.
- If the change is a Layer mask, you can move the mask to different locations for each frame, even though the mask resides in just one layer.
- If you would like to save an individual file for each frame, you can still do so fairly easily. Choose Flatten Frames into Layers from the Animation palette menu and then save each frame as a file.

Notes:

_____

_____

_____

_____

_____

_____

_____

_____

_____

_____

_____

_____

Playing and Stopping Your Animation

1. Push the Play button (the triangle) at the bottom of the Animation palette to play the animation.
2. To stop your animation from playing, push the Stop button (the square) at the bottom of the Animation palette.

Changing the Speed of Your Animation

By default, each frame will appear for 0 seconds.

1. To change the speed of an *individual* frame, activate the frame by clicking on it.
2. Click on the small arrow where it reads "0 sec."
3. Choose the speed from the presets given in the pop-up menu, or set your own time by choosing Other.
4. To change *all* the frames (*or many frames in a row*), click on the first frame you would like to change.
5. Hold the Shift key and click on the last frame you want to change.
6. Choose your desired time from the pop-up menu of any of the highlighted frames.
7. To change the delay times for *multiple, noncontiguous frames*, activate a frame you would like to change, and press Command/Ctrl and click all other desired frames.
8. Choose your desired delay time from the pop-up menu of any highlighted frame.

Notes:

_____

_____

_____

_____

_____

Changing Frame Order and Deleting Frames

To move or delete a frame:

1. Drag with your mouse to move the frame in question to the position you desire.
2. Delete a frame either by dragging it to the Trash icon in the Animation palette, or choosing Delete Frame from the palette menu.

These will affect all selected frames.

Notes:

_____

_____

_____

_____

_____

_____

_____

_____

_____

_____

_____

_____

_____

Tweening Frames

You can have ImageReady create the between-stage frames ("tween") for an animation. Here is an example based on the prior one:

1. Create the same basic image using only three layers—keep the background layer empty, have the next layer contain your shadow, and the third layer contain the ball.

2. Open the Animation palette in ImageReady. The first and only frame will show both the ball and the shadow, just like your canvas.

3. Create a new frame by clicking on the New Frame icon.

4. Activate the Move tool. Make sure that the active layer is the one that contains the ball and, holding Shift for constraint, drag the ball to the top of the canvas.

5. With Frame 2 in the Animation palette active again, activate the layer that contains the shadow within the Layer palette. Reduce the opacity of the shadow to 1%.

6. With Frame 2 still active, click the Tween button at the bottom of the Animation palette.

7. Select All Layers, since you're trying to create an animation using both the ball and the shadow.

    The next set of options is Parameters. Choose Position (for the ball) and Opacity (for the shadow).

    The third choice you'll have to make is labeled Tween With, and the options that appear within the pull-down menu will change depending on which and how many frames you have active. In this particular case, you'll want to choose Previous Frame.

    Select how many frames you want to add. The more frames you add, the more fluid your animation will look.

8. You'll see your new frames instantly added in your Animation palette, between Frames 1 and 2.

Notes:

_____

_____

Transparency and Animation

If you have transparent files and are creating an animation in which your image moves from one area to another, you will see through each frame into the one preceding it, destroying the desired moving effect.

You can keep one frame from showing through the transparent portion of the following frame(s) by "disposing" of a frame.

To set a frame disposal:

1. Make the frame(s) that you want to dispose of, or hide, active.
2. Press Command/Ctrl and click (right-mouse click in Windows) on the icon for one of the selected frames.
3. Choose Restore to Background to make the selected frames hide before the next frame appears.

Notes:

_____

_____

_____

_____

_____

_____

_____

_____

_____

_____

Optimizing an ImageReady Animation

Use the Optimize palette to set the optimization variables. All frames will assume the same settings. Images that will retain animations must be saved in the GIF file format.

The optimization settings can be a bit more involved for animations. Choose Optimize Animation from the Animation palette menu.

5. To retain only the area that has been altered from the proceeding frame, check Optimize by Bounding Box. This is checked on by default.
6. Checking Redundant Pixel Removal makes all unchanged pixels (between frames) into transparent pixels. This is also checked on by default.

Notes:

_____

_____

_____

_____

_____

_____

_____

_____

_____

_____

Saving and Opening an Animation

To save the image as a Photoshop file, choose File → Save or Save As.

Choose File → Save Optimized or Save Optimized As to save your animation as a GIF.

Notes:

_____

_____

_____

_____

_____

_____

_____

_____

_____

_____

_____

_____

_____

_____

_____

Slicing Images

"Slicing" an image means cutting up an image into smaller pieces, then reassembling them in an HTML table.

To create slices in your image:

1. In the toolbar, make the Slice tool active by clicking on it.
2. With the Slice tool, drag with your cursor to select the area where you want to make your first slice.
3. Slices generated by ImageReady are called auto-slices. Auto-slices differ in quality from the slice you created, called a user-slice. User-slices have more functionality to them.
5. Continue using the Slice tool to make further slices to your image. As you create more user-slices, more auto-slices are also created.
6. As you create slices, you will notice that each individual slice is numbered.

Notes:

_____

_____

_____

_____

_____

_____

_____

_____

_____

Selecting a Slice

1. Choose the Slice Select tool.
2. Click on the slice of your choice. If you have selected an auto-slice, that portion of your image will display in its normal color.
3. Hold the Shift key and click on another slice to select more than one at a time.
4. If you select an auto-slice, you can click in the slice and drag a selection to include multiple slices. Clicking and dragging when starting from a user-slice will move that slice elsewhere in your image. You can select all slices or deselect all slices by choosing Select → All Slice or Select → Deselect All, respectively.

Notes:

_____

_____

_____

_____

_____

_____

_____

_____

_____

_____

_____

_____

Turning an Auto-Slice Into a User-Slice

1. Select an auto-slice.
2. Choose Slice → Promote to User Slice.

Why You Would Want to Promote an Auto-Slice

Promoting auto-slices to user-slices gives you the freedom to manipulate them more freely.

Notes:

_____

_____

_____

_____

_____

_____

_____

_____

_____

_____

_____

_____

_____

Optimizing Slices

To optimize a slice, simply use the Slice Select tool and click on the slice you want to optimize. Then follow the directions for optimization.

If you want to apply the same optimization setting to more than one slice at once, you can link slices together. To link slices, select the slices you would like to link with the Select Slice tool, and choose Slice → Link Slices.

Resizing and/or Moving a Slice

1. Activate the Slice Select tool.
2. Click on the slice that you want to resize. Resize the slice by manipulating the handlebars; if you have selected an auto-slice, you will need to promote it to a user-slice.
3. If you move your slice in such a way that it overlaps another slice, ImageReady will divide the slice underneath.

Notes:

_____

_____

_____

_____

_____

_____

_____

_____

_____

Dividing a Slice

1. Select a slice.
2. From the Slice palette menu, choose Divide Slice.
3. Check the Preview checkbox.
4. Choose whether to divide your slice horizontally, vertically, or both.
5. Decide whether you want to divide your slice into equal parts or by a certain number of pixels for each division.

Combining Slices

1. Select the slices you want to combine.
2. Choose Slice → Combine Slices.

Aligning Slices With One Another

You can align slices either horizontally or vertically.

1. Select the slices you want to align. Auto-slices can't be aligned.
2. Choose Slices → Align →[your preference of alignment].

Notes:

_____

_____

_____

_____

_____

_____

_____

Using the Slice Palette

To use the Slice palette:

1. Select the type from the Type pull-down menu.
2. Select your background color from the BG pull-down menu.
3. If a particular slice is one solid color, determine its hexadecimal code. Then set the slice to No Image and access the Color Picker and fill in the hexadecimal value. This will help eliminate colors from the image and decrease download time.
4. In the Name area, you can change the file name.
5. If you want this slice to be a hyperlink, provide the appropriate Web page address in the URL text area.
6. If you use frames in your Web site (which divide your browser window into various segments) use the Target text area to specify in which frame you wish the corresponding URL to open. There are four default frame names with special meaning:
   - _blank: This will open the page in its own browser window, which will appear in front of the original one.
   - _self: This will cause the new frame to open in the same frame that held the link.
   - _parent: Loads the image in the frameset that contains the file clicked on.
   - _top: This will load your new page into the entire browser, overriding all of the frames.
7. Expand the Slice palette to include more options by choosing Show Options.
8. The Precision area allows you to control the size and position of the selected slice.
9. To maintain the original proportions, click Constrain Proportions.
10. The Message area allows you to choose what displays in the browser status area.

Saving Image Slices

To save only the image work, choose either File → Save or File → Save As.

File → Save Optimized As saves each slice as its own separate file and writes the HTML code for the <TABLE> assembly.

Notes:

_____

_____

_____

_____

_____

_____

_____

_____

_____

_____

_____

_____

_____

Creating JavaScript Rollovers

A "rollover" is an effect which happens when a Web user causes his mouse pointer to pass over an active button or link, letting him or her know that this is an active location.

Adding a Drop Shadow to the Home Button

This assumes you have an image of a button titled "Home."

1. Make the Slice Selection tool active.
2. Make sure that the slices in your image are visible.
3. Make the slice containing the word *Home* active.
4. Open the Rollover palette.
5. Create a new rollover state by clicking the New State button.
6. The new "Over" state currently looks identical to the "Normal."
7. Choose Select → Create Selection from Slice.
8. Choose Layer → New → Layer Via Copy. The word *Home* will appear in its own unique layer.
9. Because you were in the Over state when you created your new layer, that layer is only visible when the Over state is active.
10. Make the new layer active.
11. Add a drop shadow to the word *Home* by using the Layer effect Drop Shadow.
12. To see your rollover at work, Choose File → Preview In → (desired browser).

Notes:

_____

_____

_____

_____

_____

_____

A Few Other Things You Should Know

There are several other states available besides "Over":

- Down: The change will occur when the user clicks on the image.
- Click: This will change the appearance of your rollover after the user has clicked on it.
- Out: This changes the image when the user moves his or her cursor out of the rollover area.
- Up: This will change the image after the user has clicked off the image but still has his or her cursor over it.
- None: This state doesn't appear in the browser no matter what you do with your cursor—it just saves the image as it currently exists, so you can use it later.

You can also define custom JavaScript states.

Notes:

_____

_____

_____

_____

_____

_____

_____

_____

_____

Creating a Change Elsewhere in Your Image

To make a change occur elsewhere on the image, begin the same way as previously described. When you are working in the Over state, simply add the line of text or image change wherever you would like it. If it is text, it will automatically be placed in its own layer; for image changes, you will have to make your own layer. This layer will be invisible in the Normal state, and visible in the Over state.

Notes:

_____

_____

_____

_____

_____

_____

_____

_____

_____

_____

_____

_____

Triggering an Animation as a State

To make an animation begin elsewhere on the page when the user rolls his or her cursor over the Products button. Start as you did before; working in the Over state (or any other state you want to be the trigger), build your animation as described earlier in this chapter. The entire animation will be created in the chosen state.

Notes:

_____

_____

_____

_____

_____

_____

_____

_____

_____

_____

_____

_____

SUMMARY

Notes:

_____

_____

_____

_____

_____

_____

_____

_____

_____

_____

_____

_____

_____

_____

_____

_____

_____

Lecture 8 Exercises: ImageReady: Springboard to the Web

- Open the file BILLIARDS.GIF. Create an animation using all of the drawings in that file. Have the cue stick strike the white cue ball, and the cue ball break up the racked-up balls. Sink all balls, but make sure that none of them collide. Have the striped balls rotate as they move.
- Open the file EX6_3.JPG that you created in the Exercises for Lecture 6. Create JavaScript rollovers for each button.
- Open the file EX7_2.JPG that you created in the Exercises for Lecture 7. Slice this image for use on a Web site.

Lecture Nine

Real-Life Example: A Complete Walkthrough

Objectives:

- Preview Lecture 9

- Create the Example Logo

- Create the Example Titlebar and Background

- Design the Example Buttons

- Slice and Link the Buttons

- Create the Button Rollovers

- Review Lecture 9

This chapter will walk you through the creation of a Web site for Union County Flower Supply (UCFS).

The Client
At the point that we were contacted, UCFS had no real database for their products, no brand identity that we needed to adhere to, giving us an open canvas to play with.

The Market
The first step was to understand the market. The current customer base was mostly business people; UCFS would like to extend that to the end user as well.

The Brand
The company name sounded local; for the Web brand, we chose to create a brand name that didn't sound so limited and permitted sub-branding of products (Efloralz.com with products like EBasketz and EBalloonz).

Notes:

_____

_____

_____

_____

_____

_____

_____

_____

132   KYLE'S PHOTOSHOP WORKBOOK

Variable Constraints

When designing a Web site, there are some constraints which you will not have control over. In this case, the company has a Web host which supports only a specific shopping cart program; thus we can't design our own specific interface and shopping cart program. Other similar constraints can appear, such as a decree from one of the customer's executives as to the look he prefers, or a limitation on the bandwidth they want to support, and so on.

Intent of Use

This was not going to be a site for a lot of "window shopping" because the main clientele were business people. If the products were too hard to find, the customers would just give up, and likely never come back.

Notes:

_____

_____

_____

_____

_____

_____

_____

_____

_____

_____

War on Design

Artists and designers like to have things that are pretty, often elaborate, and which satisfy their artistic tastes. Marketing and usability people prefer clean, simple, and straightforward. In general, marketing and usability should win out in this area, although some allowance should be made to permit the designers to create a unique and attractive look. Only sites which have a good reason to make a point of their artistic and Web-savvy talent need to use the cutting-edge extremes.

Navigational Hierarchy

As suggested in earlier chapters, always work out the hierarchy on paper before trying to create it online. For our example:

The Home page, at the top of what looks like a pyramid, is the page where people enter the site. From that page, they are able to go directly to any number of other pages, including the sub-branded pages; entering one of the sub-brands, or second-tier pages, gives you access to certain other third-tier pages. Each needs to contain easy access to the other pages that are associated with it.

The Layout

Also as suggested previously, the navigation material was placed along the top and lefthand sides. A constant site logo will be on every page.

Notes:

_____

_____

_____

_____

_____

The Logo

The logo chosen makes use of rounded corners and angled outlines for effect, but concentrates on bold fonts to display the name of the site with extreme clarity. The tag line was worked into the overall logo for one cohesive billboard.

The logo was created in the following manner:

1. Opened a canvas 288 x 144 pixels, RGB, 300 ppi. They immediately created a new layer, Layer 1, to work on and saved the file as "logo.psd." The logo was created at high resolution because it may also be used on printed materials (shipping forms and letterhead, for instance) and it's always easier to reduce resolution than increase it later.

2. On Layer 1, the main billboard was made. Rounded edges made it somewhat difficult to make; the Shape tool combined with a Free Transform command was tried but the result wasn't satisfactory.

3. With the Polygonal Lasso tool activated, a selection was made in the general shape desired; the designer then opened the Channels palette and pushed the New Channel icon.

4. The selection was feathered (Select → Feather) by 10 pixels, causing the corners to look rounded. The selection was then filled with white.

5. The image was deselected.

6. Accessing Image → Adjust → Levels, the shadows and highlights were brought to the center until they overlapped with the midtones marker, hardening the selection edge.

7. A selection was made of the white area by pressing Command (Ctrl in Windows) and clicking on the active channel, and then it was loaded back into the main composite by activating the RGB channel.

8. The Gradient tool was used to transition the color in the selection from light green at the top to a darker shade at the bottom.

9. The Drop Shadow Layer attribute was accessed; a slight drop shadow with a significant blur was applied below and to the right of the image.

10. The Type tool was activated, and the designer clicked on the far left of the banner. A new Text layer was automatically created, and the "Efloralz.com" lettering was placed.

11. A new layer was created and placed below the text layer. With this new layer active, a selection was made of the text.

12. One of the selection tools was activated and the selection was nudged two pixels to the right and two pixels down and filled with black.

13. A very light drop shadow was created with layer attributes.

14. A new layer for the tag line was created and placed above the text layer. The rounded-corner Shape tool was used with a light color in the foreground.

15. The Stroke Layer attribute was used to place a dark outline around the shape, and the drop shadow that was originally placed was copied and pasted onto the pill-shape layer.

16. "Your Virtual Floral Department Store" was placed in the pill shape.

All of the layers except the background were linked together and merged into one layer. The end result was two layers—the logo and the background layer.

The Titlebar/Background

It was in the making of the titlebar that the required shopping-cart program caused problems. The original concept involved using frames, but the shopping-cart program didn't work well with frames. To deal with this required a trick involving a very, very large background image (large so as to accommodate virtually any size product list).

1. With a new canvas, 1,200 x 5,000 pixels, a new layer was created directly over the background layer.

2. The Ellipse marquee tool and the Rectangular marquee tool were combined to make the curved upper titlebar. First the canvas was changed to be in Full View mode; then it was zoomed out until the whole canvas was displayed.

3. Using the Ellipse marquee tool, an oval selection was created toward the top left of the canvas, so that the left downward slope of the oval was running off the canvas and into the gray work area.

4. With the rulers open, a horizontal guide was created at the very top of the oval; the tool was changed to the Rectangular mar-

quee. With the Shift key held down, a rectangular selection was created, with the top left corner of the rectangle made at the point where the ruler meets the top of the oval. This rectangular selection was extended to the far right edge of the canvas.

5. The selection was inverted.

6. The selection was filled with the lavender shade we chose.

7. The Elliptical marquee tool was reactivated. While pressing the Option, Alt and the Shift key, a large circle was created to encompass about 40% of the upper margin, starting from the right side. The remaining selection was the intersection between the selection that existed and the large circle that was just made.

8. The current selection was filled with a darker purple, and a Drop Shadow Layer attribute applied to create a very slight drop shadow.

9. From a stock image photo library, a picture of a flower on a plain white background was chosen, the Magic Wand tool was used to select the white, and then the selection was inverted, giving just the flower, which was added to the titlebar.

10. The logo canvas was reactivated and, with the logo layer active, the Move tool was used to drag the logo onto the background canvas we just created. The logo was automatically placed in its own layer and positioned into place on the titlebar.

Since the background was so large, we would want to make the background transparent. However, the drop shadows made this not quite so easy – you cannot have conditional transparency. Instead, the background layer was filled first with the selected color, the layers flattened, and the Magic Eraser used to make the body of the background transparent without affecting the background under the logo and upper bar.

The image was saved as a GIF using Save for Web.

The Buttons, Step 1: Creating the Design

In an entirely new document, the Shape tool (the one with the rounded corners) was used to create the initial button on its own layer. It was then selected and a gradient of light green to darker green was applied. A purple stroke was created around the edge with Edit → Stroke.

This was duplicated eight times to create a vertical column of buttons.

With the column of buttons in place, the name of each button was created on its own layer, directly above its respective button, and then merged with that button. Similarly the images associated with each button were placed above and merged with their buttons. The file was saved as a Photoshop document.

The Buttons, Step 2: Slicing and Linking

As described in Lecture 8, the now-saved Button Bar was pulled up in ImageReady and sliced. Its background layer was made transparent to permit the prior background to show. As each Sliced button was selected, it was given the URL it was to link to with the Slice palette.

The Buttons, Step 3: Rollover States

Using the techniques detailed in Lecture 8, the buttons were all given a drop shadow and bevel for the "Over" state, thus creating a rollover. For backup the buttons were saved as-is, and then Optimized and saved under another name.

Putting the Rest of the Site Together

As is common, the information in the middle of the pages was intended to change/update often, but consisted of text and images. This was assembled in DreamWeaver with additions of ImageReady code where needed.

SUMMARY

Notes:

_____

_____

_____

_____

_____

Lecture 9 Exercies: Real-Life Example: A Complete Walkthrough

5. Using the Web site and associated concepts created in this lecture as a guide, create a similar Web site home page, except the client in this case will be the eNotes musical instrument e-tailer. Use the music-related files that you have created in previous lecture Exercises for your graphics.